Natural Landmarks

RENNAY CRAATS

WEIGL PUBLISHERS INC.

Project Coordinator
Tina Schwartzenberger

Design
Janine Vangool

Layout
Bryan Pezzi

Substantive Editor
Heather C. Hudak

Copy Editor
Heather Kissock

Photo Researcher
Wendy Cosh

Published by Weigl Publishers Inc.
350 5th Avenue, Suite 3304
New York, NY USA 10118-0069
Web site: www.weigl.com

Library of Congress Cataloging-in-Publication Data

Craats, Rennay.
  Natural landmarks / Rennay Craats.
     p. cm. -- (American symbols)
Includes index.
Summary: A simple introduction to such natural landmarks as Old Faithful and Niagara Falls, including their history, beauty, importance in tourism, and other facts.
  ISBN 1-59036-133-4 (Library Bound : alk. paper)
 1. Natural history--United States--Juvenile literature. 2. Natural monuments--United States--Juvenile literature. [1. Natural history. 2. Natural monuments. 3. Landforms.] I. Title. II. American symbols (Mankato, Minn.)
  QH104.C73 2003
  508.73--dc21

                                        2003005034

Printed in the United States of America
1 2 3 4 5 6 7 8 9 0   07 06 05 04 03

Photograph Credits
Every reasonable effort has been made to trace ownership and to obtain permission to reprint copyright material. The publishers would be pleased to have any errors or omissions brought to their attention so that they may be corrected in subsequent printings.

Cover: The Grand Canyon (CORBIS/MAGMA/Royalty-Free); **Cave of the Mounds:** page 17T; **CORBIS/MAGMA:** pages 12/13, 13R, 16B (Douglas Peebles), 17M (Royalty-Free), 17B (Richard Hamilton Smith); **Corel Corporation:** pages 6/7, 7T, 10/11, 11T, 22; **Clint Farlinger:** page 15M; **Debbie Hall:** page 16M; **Bruce Leighty:** pages 1, 15B; **Steve Mulligan:** pages 4B, 8/9, 9T; **National Park Service:** pages 3, 4T, 5, 14M; **Photos.com:** pages 14T, 23; **Bruno Smid:** page 15T; **Jim Steinhart of www.PlanetWare.com:** page 14B; **Arieh Tal NTTL Photo:** page 16T; **Kristen Uri:** page 21.

Contents

★ Introduction 4

★ The Grand Canyon 6

★ Niagara Falls 8

★ Florida Everglades 10

★ Old Faithful 12

★ Landmarks to Know 14

★ Landmarks Everywhere 18

★ Landmarks of the U.S.A. 20

★ Further Research 22

★ Explore a Landmark 23

★ Glossary 24

★ Index 24

Introduction

The United States is filled with natural landmarks. Some draw millions of visitors each year. Others are best known to the people who live nearby. Large or small, natural landmarks across the United States are beautiful and exciting places to visit. These areas are important to U.S. citizens. For this reason, the government has created laws to protect many natural landmarks, making sure these places will be around for years to come.

Few plants and animals can survive in the harsh conditions of White Sands National Park in New Mexico.

Millions of tourists go to New York state to visit Niagara Falls each year. Visitors can view the falls from observation towers, boats, or parks along the Niagara River.

Natural landmarks offer more than stunning scenery. They are symbols that represent a specific region or state. A symbol is an item that stands for something else. Some of the most popular natural landmarks include the Grand Canyon, Niagara Falls, the Florida Everglades, and Old Faithful.

Many unusual rock shapes fill Utah's Arches National Park.

The Grand Canyon

The Grand Canyon is found in northwestern Arizona. Every day, tourists from the United States and around the world visit the canyon. The massive canyon is 277 miles long and as wide as 18 miles in some places. The steep walls drop more than 5,000 feet down into the canyon.

The Grand Canyon began to form about 6 million years ago. The area's dry soil could not absorb water. When it rained, water rushed down the valleys into the Colorado River, which flows through the lower part of the canyon. Over the years, this caused **erosion,** forming the cliffs and valleys of the Grand Canyon.

There are three distinct sections in the Grand Canyon National Park: the South Rim, the North Rim, and the Inner Canyon. Each section has its own climate and plant life.

From the canyon's top to the bottom, nine rock layers stack like pancakes. The top layer is limestone rock that dates back about 250 million years. The rocks on the bottom layer are between 500 million and 1 billion years old. Its age makes the Grand Canyon a great place to learn about geology and nature. This incredible natural landmark is both a national park and a national monument.

★ More than 4 million people travel to the Grand Canyon National Park each year. Many visitors hike and camp on the rocky landscape of the canyon.

★ The temperature in the canyon can grow very cold. Water freezes in cracks between rocks. When water freezes, it expands and forces the rock apart. As the cracks grow, rock close to the edge breaks away from the canyon. Over time, this process has helped to form the Grand Canyon.

★ In 1963, the Glen Canyon Dam was built. The dam slowed the flow of sand down the Colorado River into the canyon. In 1996, the government opened the dam to release more than 100 billion gallons of water into the canyon. This helped clear **sediment** and **debris** from the area where fish go to lay their eggs.

★ Europeans first wrote about the Grand Canyon in 1540. Since it was so difficult to travel to the canyon, it was nearly 300 years before this landmark was explored.

Niagara Falls

Each year, millions of people are drawn to visit the incredible power and beauty of Niagara Falls. The falls borders two countries. Horseshoe Falls flows on the Canadian side. The American Falls is located in New York on the United States side. The American Falls flows 182 feet down and is 1,075 feet wide. Niagara Falls's volume of water flow can generate a great deal of power. Power plants use the water's force and energy to produce nearly 2.5 million kilowatts of electricity on the U.S. side, and another 2 million kilowatts on the Canadian side.

About 500 years ago, the Niagara River split into two around Goat Island. As a result, two distinct sets of falls were created. The two falls are the Horseshoe Falls and the American Falls, pictured below.

Niagara Falls was formed more than 12,000 years ago when water from Lake Erie began to rush over the Niagara **Escarpment**. The location of the falls slowly moved upstream as land beneath the water eroded. Niagara Falls continues to erode at a rate of about 5 feet per year on the Canadian side and about 6 inches annually on the U.S. side.

★ Niagara Falls is home to the world's first large **hydroelectric** generating station. It was built in 1895.

★ The Horseshoe Falls are larger than the American Falls. Nine times more water moves over the Horseshoe Falls than the American Falls.

★ The Horseshoe and American Falls are separated by Goat Island, New York.

★ In 1969, a dam stopped the flow of water at the American Falls for several months. This gave scientists time to study the land beneath the moving water.

★ In 1894, French Emperor Napoleon Bonaparte's brother brought his bride to the falls. Since then, Niagara Falls has been a popular place to have a honeymoon or wedding.

Florida Everglades

The Florida Everglades is a mysterious natural landmark. The Everglades was formed when water flowing from the Kissimmee River caused shallow Lake Okeechobee to overflow. As a result, ponds, **sloughs**, marshes, and **uplands** formed. Found on the southern tip of Florida, the Everglades is the only **subtropical preserve** in North America. To protect this area, the government created the Everglades National Park in 1947. This park covers 1.5 million acres of land and water. About half of this area is freshwater. In fact, the Everglades is really a slow-moving river. It covers about 5,000 square miles of land. The Everglades is about 50 miles wide, but only 6 inches deep on average.

The Florida Everglades is lined with mangrove and cypress trees. It is also home to many types of animals. Alligators live in the swampy waters of the Everglades. Alligators in this area can grow quite large. Visitors who take boat tours in the park are warned to keep away from these dangerous animals. The mosquito is the most common creature found in the Everglades. Forty-three different types of mosquito live there. Rare animals also live in this area. Some of these animals, such as the manatee, are **endangered**. To protect the animals and the threatened wetland area, the Florida Everglades has been named a World Heritage Site, and a Wetland of International Importance. This means that the Everglades are protected worldwide.

Plants and animals in the Everglades are used to alternating wet and dry seasons. Changes in the water cycle can ruin feeding and nesting conditions.

★ The largest alligator ever seen in Florida was 17 feet, 5 inches long.

★ Water levels in the Florida Everglades are affected by rain that falls between May and October. Most of the rain **evaporates** or is **absorbed** by plants.

★ The Everglades is the only place on Earth where alligators and crocodiles live together.

★ Today, 50 percent of South Florida's original wetland areas no longer exist. As a result, some animal populations are at risk of disappearing.

Old Faithful

Old Faithful is one of the world's most famous geysers. Geysers are natural underground springs that shoot water and steam into the air. A geyser erupts when hot volcanic rocks heat water inside the earth, causing the water to boil and steam. The boiling water expands, pushing some of the water and steam up into the air. Old Faithful is found in Yellowstone National Park. The park covers northwestern Wyoming and parts of Idaho and Montana.

Only a few geysers are known to erupt at **predictable** times. Old Faithful is one such geyser. On average, it erupts about once every 80 minutes. Sometimes eruptions occur as often as 45 minutes apart. Each eruption lasts between 1 and 5 minutes. It is this predictability that gave Old Faithful its name. Old Faithful shoots 10,000 to 12,000 gallons of boiling water into the air each time it erupts. The stream of water can reach 106 to 184 feet into the sky. Two million people visit Yellowstone National Park each year. Many of them come to watch Old Faithful erupt.

Old Faithful is located in the Upper Geyser Basin of Yellowstone National Park. One-quarter of the world's geysers are located in this 2-square-mile area.

★ Old Faithful is well known, but it is not the largest geyser in Yellowstone National Park. Grand Geyser is the world's largest geyser. It is also the most predictable geyser in the park. It erupts for 9 to 12 minutes every 7 to 15 hours.

★ In 1998, an earthquake increased the time between Old Faithful's eruptions by 4 minutes. This was caused by a shift in the land.

★ Yellowstone National Park is home to about 10,000 bubbling mud pots, hot springs, geysers, and steaming pools. Most of the world's geysers are located near Old Faithful.

Landmarks to Know

From rivers to rock formations, natural landmarks are everywhere. Many fascinating examples of nature can be found across the United States.

★ Utah Arches

More than 1,000 colorful arches are found in eastern Utah's Arches National Park. Some arches are only 3 feet across. Others are very large, measuring about 300 feet across. Erosion has carved these sandstone arches. Wind and underground water chipped away at the sandstone creating huge stone archways and towers. The Landscape Arch stands in a part of the park named Devil's Garden. It is the world's longest natural arch, measuring 306 feet across.

★ White Sands

The Chihuahuan Desert in New Mexico contains miles of shimmering white sand. The White Sands National Monument was created to protect this natural wonder. The white sands are **gypsum dunes**. White Sands National Monument is the world's largest gypsum dune field. The dunes cover 275 square miles of desert. Very little wildlife survives here.

★ Badlands

Badlands National Park in southwestern South Dakota covers 242,756 acres of land. The park is covered with unique rock formations. The rocks form oddly shaped hills and steep valleys. Years of low rainfall followed by a long **drought** led to erosion in the area. The erosion caused ridges, canyons, and **buttes** to form. There are even **fossil** remains in the rocks.

★ Madison Boulder

Located in New Hampshire, Madison Boulder is a huge rock that rises from the ground. It is 83 feet long, 23 feet high, and 37 feet wide. Madison Boulder was dragged to its current location by a giant sheet of ice called a glacier. Rocks that have been moved in this way are called erratics. Madison Boulder is one of the largest erratics in the world. In 1970, Madison Boulder was made a National Natural Landmark.

★ Mississippi River

The Mississippi River forms most of the western border of Mississippi state. The Mississippi River flows across most of the United States and empties into the Gulf of Mexico. From Lake Itasca in Minnesota to the Gulf of Mexico, the Mississippi River measures about 2,340 miles long. It is the largest and most important river in North America. The Mississippi River is used to transport goods and people. It carries more goods and people than any other inland body of water on the continent.

★ Mount Saint Helens

Mount Saint Helens is a well-known active volcano in Washington state. In 1980, Mount Saint Helens erupted for the first time since 1857. The eruption began when a column of **magma** started pushing up inside the mountain. An earthquake caused a landslide on the mountain. The landslide triggered a volcanic eruption. Gases and a cloud of ash shot 12 miles into the air. The eruption killed 57 people. The volcano also became shorter after the eruption. It shrank from 9,677 feet to 8,365 feet. People often visit Mount Saint Helens to see this powerful volcano.

★ Bartholomew's Cobble

Bartholomew's Cobble in Massachusetts is a 329-acre natural landmark. The area is home to more than 800 types of plants and 240 kinds of birds. Six miles of trails lead through woods, forest, and meadow. The area was named for two rocky hills that rise above the Housatonic River. The hills are made up of limestone and marble stones called cobbles. Bartholomew's Cobble became a National Natural Landmark in 1971.

★ Ginkgo Petrified Forest

More than 200 species of trees that have turned to stone can be found in the Ginkgo Petrified Forest State Park. About 15 million years ago, this part of Washington state was covered by lakes and swamps. Erupting volcanoes covered logs and tree limbs that had sunk to the bottoms of lakes and swamps with hot lava. The lava hardened around the logs and petrified them, or turned them to stone. The 7,500-acre park has petrified wood from the rare Ginkgo tree, a tree that no longer grows in the wild.

★ Mauna Kea

Hawai'i's Mauna Kea is the highest mountain in the world. Even though Hawai'i is known for its year-round hot weather, Mauna Kea is covered by snow during the winter months. This peak is actually a volcano. It measures about 32,000 feet from its base on the ocean floor to its tip. Mauna Kea has not erupted for 3,500 years. Scientists believe that Mauna Kea will erupt again one day.

★ Cave of the Mounds

Cave of the Mounds is located in Wisconsin. This limestone cave has a 20-foot-tall opening that leads to other chambers. Water, air, and carbon dioxide combined to create incredible formations on the cave floor and ceiling. Miners removing limestone rock from a **quarry** discovered the cave when a dynamite blast revealed a great underground tunnel. **Stalactites** hung down from the ceiling, and **stalagmites** grew from the floor.

★ Mount McKinley

North America's highest mountain is found in Alaska's Denali National Park and Preserve. Mount McKinley towers 20,320 feet above sea level. Native Peoples called the mountain *Denali*, which means "The High One." In 1896, the mountain was renamed after President William McKinley. Mount McKinley slopes 17,000 feet along a distance of only 12 miles. It is said to be one of the steepest vertical climbs in the world. Many people try to reach the peak of Mount McKinley, but most fail. The steep slope and harsh weather stop climbers from reaching the top of this great mountain.

★ Painted Desert

Arizona is home to the Painted Desert. A rainbow of colored rock covers about 7,500 square miles of land along the Little Colorado River. Red, blue, purple, yellow, brown, and gray rock formations fill the desert. Fossils that date back millions of years are also found in the rocks. The land is made up of soft sandstone, mud, and volcanic ash. The landscape of the Painted Desert has as much variety as it does color. Buttes, cliffs, slopes, and **mesas** attract visitors to this natural landmark.

Landmarks Everywhere

The United States has many natural landmarks. This map shows where each of the 16 natural landmarks featured in this book are located. Are any of these natural landmarks near you?

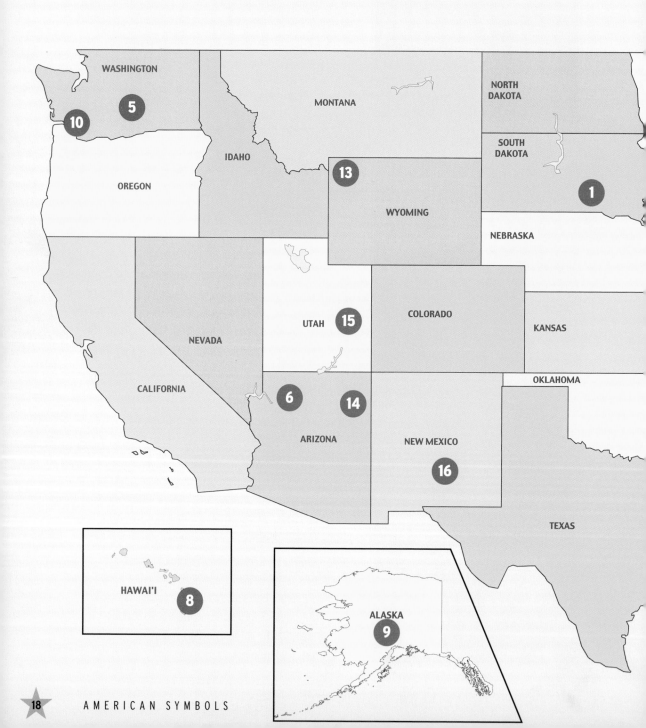

AMERICAN SYMBOLS

1. **Badlands**: South Dakota
2. **Bartholomew's Cobble**: Massachusetts
3. **Cave of the Mounds**: Wisconsin
4. **Everglades**: Florida
5. **Ginkgo Petrified Forest**: Washington

6. **Grand Canyon**: Arizona
7. **Madison Boulder**: New Hampshire
8. **Mauna Kea**: Hawai'i
9. **Mount McKinley**: Alaska
10. **Mount Saint Helens**: Washington
11. **Mississippi River**: runs throughout central U.S.

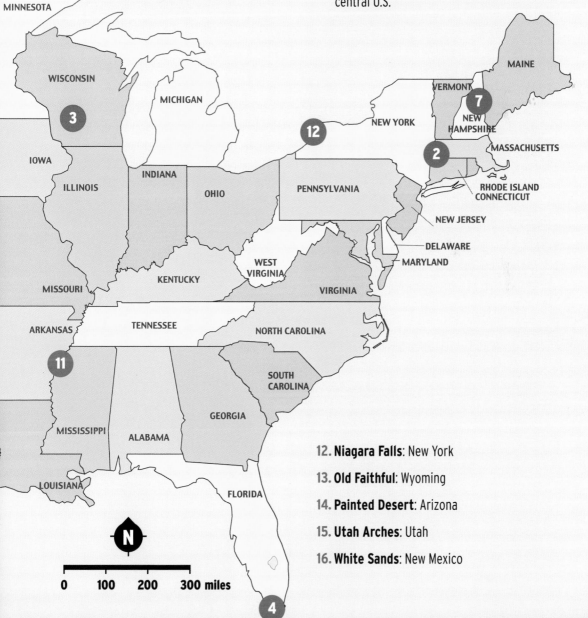

12. **Niagara Falls**: New York
13. **Old Faithful**: Wyoming
14. **Painted Desert**: Arizona
15. **Utah Arches**: Utah
16. **White Sands**: New Mexico

Landmarks of the U.S.A.

The sixteen natural landmarks in this book represent only a few natural formations found across the United States. This chart lists several more. Are any located in your state?

LANDMARK	STATE
Ancient River Warren Channel	Minnesota
Big Cypress Bend	Florida
Bitter Lake Swamp	New Mexico
Cleveland-Lloyd Dinosaur Quarry	Utah
Devil's Canyon	Oklahoma
Ell Pond	Rhode Island
Enchanted Rock	Texas
Franklin Bog	Vermont
Gay Heads Cliff	Massachusetts
Gilpin's Falls	Maryland
Glacial Lake Missoula	Montana
Grand Coulee	Washington
Grapevine Mesa Joshua Trees	Arizona
Great Rift System	Idaho
Hanging Rock and Wabash Reef	Indiana
Hart's Woods	New York
Luray Caverns	Virginia
Mammoth Spring	Arkansas
Marshall Forest–Georgia Mississippi Palisades	Illinois
Nebraska Sand Hills	Nebraska
New Gloucester Black Gum Stand	Maine
Point Beach Ridges	Wisconsin

The Valley of Fire State Park is located near Las Vegas, Nevada. Nevada's oldest state park, it contains sandstone formations and sand dunes more than 150 million years old.

Porcupine Mountain	Michigan
Red River Gorge	Kentucky
Saint Phillips Island	South Carolina
Slumgullion Earthflow	Colorado
Tamarack Swamp	Pennsylvania
The Castles	South Dakota
Troy Meadows	New Jersey
Two Ocean Pass	Wyoming
Valley of Fire	Nevada
Willamette Floodplain	Oregon
Walrus Islands	Alaska

Further Research

The United States is home to many natural landmarks. The Internet and your local library are great places to find more information about these landmarks and how they were formed. These Web sites and books can help you learn more.

Visitors can fly over the Grand Canyon in helicopters and airplanes. They can also raft down the Colorado River for a different view of the canyon.

Web Sites

★ To find out about registered landmarks, visit the National Natural Landmark Registry at: www.nature.nps.gov/nnl/Registry/USA_Map

★ For more information about the Grand Canyon, visit: www.grand.canyon.national-park.com

★ Find out more about Niagara Falls at: www.niagarafallsstatepark.com

★ To view pictures and read more information about Old Faithful, visit: www.oldfaithfulgeyser.com

Books

★ Fisher, Leonard Everett. *Niagara Falls.* New York: Holiday House, 1996

★ Yolen, Jane. *Welcome to the River of Grass.* New York: G.P. Putnam Publishing Group, 2001

Explore a Landmark

Nearly every state has at least one registered national natural landmark. All 50 states have natural areas. Research the natural areas in your state. Make a list of these natural areas. Next, choose one natural landmark that interests you. Write a paragraph describing the area. How was it formed? What are its features? Be descriptive so that other people will want to visit your favorite area.

You may choose to research a waterfall near your hometown.

Glossary

★ **absorbed:** taken in or soaked up

★ **buttes:** steep-sided hills

★ **debris:** scattered, broken pieces

★ **drought:** period of dry weather

★ **endangered:** animals whose populations are so low that they are in danger of disappearing completely

★ **erosion:** gradual wearing away

★ **escarpment:** a steep slope at the edge of a plateau

★ **evaporates:** when water turns into vapor

★ **fossil:** remains of plants or animals that have hardened into rock

★ **gypsum dunes:** chalk-like minerals in the shape of a small hill

★ **hydroelectric:** electric power made from water

★ **magma:** molten rock beneath Earth's surface

★ **mesas:** high plateaus with steep sides

★ **predictable:** something that happens as it is expected to

★ **quarry:** an open pit from which stone or other material is extracted, usually by blasting, cutting, or drilling

★ **sediment:** minerals deposited by water

★ **sloughs:** swamps or marshes

★ **stalactites:** icicle-shaped deposits that hang from a cave roof

★ **stalagmites:** deposits that stand like a pillar from a cave floor

★ **subtropical preserve:** area of nearly tropical land

★ **uplands:** areas of higher land

Index

alligators 10, 11

arches 5, 14, 18, 19

dunes 14, 21

erosion 6, 9, 14

eruption 12, 13, 15, 16

Florida Everglades 5, 10, 11, 19

geyser 12, 13

Grand Canyon 5, 6, 7, 18, 19, 22

marshes 10

Mississippi River 15, 19

monument 7, 14

Niagara Falls 4, 5, 8, 9, 19, 22

Old Faithful 5, 12, 13, 18, 19, 22

sandstone 14, 17, 21

volcano 15, 16

Yellowstone National Park . . . 12, 13